Playing outside

We are going to play

on the swings.

We like playing

on the swings.

We are going to play
in the tunnel.

We like playing

in the tunnel.

We are going to play
on the slide.

We like playing

on the slide.

We are going to play
in the tent.

We like playing

in the tent.